Romeo, Romeo ... Fetch Us Thy Manners!

by Juliet and Romeo

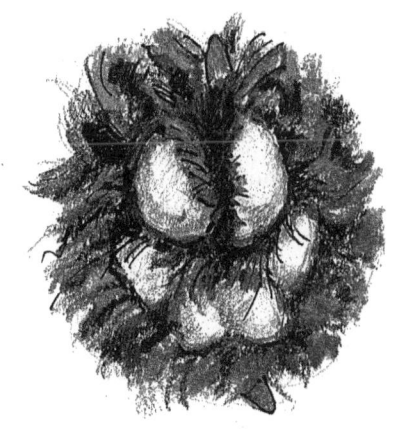

Romeo, Romeo . . . Fetch Us Thy Manners!
Written and Illustrated by Louise Elerding
MannersA2Z@aol.com

Copyright © 2017 Louise Elerding

ISBN: 978-1-938620-19-5
Cataloging-in-Publication data for this book
is available from the Library of Congress

Westcom Press, LLC
10736 Jeffersion Boulevard
Suite 383
Culver City, CA 90230

Westcom.Press@mac.com

All rights reserved. No part of this publication may be reproduced or transmitted in any form or by any means, electronic or mechanical, including photocopying, recording, or by any information storage or retrieval system, without permission in writing from the publisher.

Printed in the United States of America
21 20 19 18 17   1 2 3 4 5

For bulk purchase pricing for fundraising, animal rights organizations, and other nonprofits, please contact: MannersA2Z@aol.com

TABLE OF CONTENTS

Dedication vii
Acknowledgements ix
Introduction xi
Socializing~Mannerizing 1
We Yearn to Learn and Earn.. 9
Spare Us a Scolding 15
Just Once 21
Raise the Praise 27
Four on the Floor 33
Fashionable, Functional Neckwear 39
Wait at the Gate and Door... 45
A Message of Friendly 51
Sidewalk Garden-Pardons 55
Polite Compromises 61
Hark the Bark 65
Cheers for Ears.. 69
Doggy Dining Etiquette 75
Apartment Pooches 81
Brainy Games 87
Out into the Big World... 93
About the Coauthors.. 101

DEDICATION

To our canine friends who adore their humans, and our human friends and family who cherish their dogs. We all know the joys of pet relationships and how they enrich our lives to the fullest. Cheers to the life lessons and love we've shared in this arena!

ACKNOWLEDGEMENTS

To my special crew who did a preview/reading with eyes wide open: Alicia, Annette, Diana, Joanie, Marj, and Susie.

To my supportive daughters Alyson and Kristin, who gave an enthusiastic thumb up to the re-opening of my illustration toolbox.

To Michael Vezo and J. McCrary, my publishing/editing team, whose brilliance and clarity never falter.

INTRODUCTION

Woof—hi! My name is Romeo, and I'm a black Standard Poodle. My registered name is Romeo Mon Ami, which translates from the French as "Romeo, my friend."

We Standard Poodles are companion dogs—all we want is to be at our masters' side and to be their best friend.

We are not interested in jumping fences to get away, or hunting down ducks or other critters, or herding cattle or sheep. We just want to be a good sidekick, play, socialize with a lot of people and other dogs, be helpful, and cuddle often. In my world, being treated like a dog means love, friendship, and a wonderful life.

My part-time job of being a Manners Messenger comes from my Poodle heritage of wanting to be around people all the time. I'm writing this book to share some easy manner tips with you and your own dog, and to help make your lives together even better than it is now.

I know dogs with good manners attract more friends and many more welcoming hugs, pettings, and human playmates. Humans say that when we pups are well behaved, we are proud of ourselves, and life is even more glorious for family and friends alike.

Juliet is my master, my trainer, and my coauthor. She and I invite you to be a virtual member of the Polite Team of the Canine World. It's fun, it's easy, and it's very rewarding to be mannerly.

Here we go! Woof–woof . . . hooray!

Socializing~Mannerizing

Socialization and good manners are practically synonymous. Like good friends, they go paw-in-paw. We canines need structure—routines, consistent patterns, and *lots* of love from our humans. A structured environment encourages us to want to bond and please.

Experiencing socialization gives us the opportunity to be very well-rounded, happy, well-behaved dogs—the kind of pets that people enjoy being around. *Polite* pets!

Lucky are we who were brought into this world by aware breeders and families, those who gave us vital puppy-development skills. Dogs without the benefit of early socialization can still benefit from similar experiences as older dogs.

Nature's plan is awesome, as our birth moms and littermates have key lessons for us during our first eight weeks of development. The positive outcome is beyond belief.

Socializing~Mannerizing

During my first two weeks of life, my mother Daisy was my whole world. She was a great mom: calm, devoted to me and my littermates. The breeder hadn't bred her too often, and this kept her healthy and eager to parent us.

We puppies are born blind and deaf, so my mom's instincts were paramount. Right away, I learned the sense of touch and taste from her, which led me to nurse her. She kept us cuddled together to keep us warm, because puppies' body temperature is critical to survival.

During week two, my ears perked up and I began hearing sounds. I could smell new smells, my eyes opened to the light around me, and I felt something hard poking through my gums. I already had little teeth! The most fun was when I began to stand, then I walked on my feet, my tail wagged, and sounds came out of my mouth. I was barking. My mom and my six littermates were my biggest influence.

Then came week three, and I began to bounce and play more. Being with people and dogs and having relationships taught me about being more independent. The breeders showed me my first toys, and I really liked that! Even a cardboard box can be exciting to climb into. Toys taught me to not be afraid of new or strange objects.

By week four, I learned even more about being a dog. I began eating solid food. My birth-parents, Matix and Daisy, taught us to feel confident in being pups, as we watched their role modeling. I imitated them and was a happy little follower, with my tail held upright, a sign of being content and well-adjusted. People began holding me and cuddling me, and I was learning to love humans.

Weeks four to six, I continued to learn to play, developed some new social skills, and, very importantly, I learned about the inhibited bite. This is a critical step, as I

Socializing~Mannerizing

learned social boundaries and hierarchy from my mom, brothers, and sisters. For all dogs throughout their lives, the inhibited bite is a form of friendship, playtime, and bonding.

At week five, my breeders (the grownups and their three children) began to have significant influence on me as my littermates and I developed more interaction with humans. They thought we were so adorable! I confidently began exploring and snooping, and developed a healthy curiosity.

By week seven, I began to fine-tune my coordination and physical abilities. My breeder began introducing me to the idea of house training, which I was beginning to understand. My mom had already taught me not to potty where I sleep—an important beginning.

Then came week eight, and I was getting prepared to go to my new home soon. I felt some independence and could also tell it was normal that some new things frightened me at this stage, so I had very supportive humans to reassure me that everything would be okay. And it was!

In the weeks and months to follow, I enjoyed growing up healthy, social, affectionate, and happy. I attribute my ability to adapt well to my loving, normal, and well-cared-for beginning. I was eager to learn to be a well-mannered companion and pooch.

Every day of my life, since I came to live in my new home when I was nine weeks old, my master takes my face in her hands, kisses me on the head, and tells me, *You are the best boy in the whole wide world, and I love you to pieces.* That's being loving and mannerly—all bundled up together. It's better than the cat's meow.

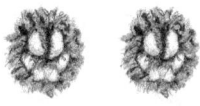

A happy note: On the day that I dotted the last "i" and crossed the last "t" of this manuscript, I met one of my littermates for the first time since I left my mom. We had tracked each other down, and my brother Calvin and I met on the Sunday of Memorial Weekend, surely a memorable day for all of us.

Since Calvin and I will be three years old this July, we saw each other full grown and almost fully mature. We look like twins, and even have the same small white mark on our chests. I am about 10 pounds lighter than he is and maybe an inch shorter. We share the same prance, eyes, and bark.

Our humans agreed unanimously that we recognized each other from our litter days.

Calvin's master noted that she has never seen him respond to other new dogs with this much intimacy and calmness. We stayed close by each other, romping, playing, doing our inhibited bites, and touching noses and faces continuously, just like we did in our early, comfy litter-pen.

This was a love-day reunion.

We Yearn to Learn and Earn

Dogs love to please our humans! We feel very good about ourselves when given an opportunity to shine.

We pups thrive on rules and routines, and we happily learn to follow your consistent commands.

Learning and earning is a forever part of our life. The day I left my birth-family and arrived at this home, a new learning curve began.

I am required to *earn* everything I receive—which also reminds me who's the boss. This is important, because it means my master and I are exchanging levels of respect.

When it's time for a meal, I must sit calmly before I can be fed. For a toy, I may be asked to shake hands to earn it. It's always "humans first" when going through a door, so I wait and follow. When houseguests arrive, I must sit nicely to greet them. At treat time, I may be asked to perform another trick or respond to a new command.

My black lab playmate, Missy, who watches over me like a big sister, had to leave a newspaper untouched on the end table one whole day, and that earned her a special dinner treat that evening.

Dogs can also learn hand signals, used either together with a word command or used solo. Sometimes it comes in handy to have a way to communicate without words.

When my master wants me to come to her, she often slaps her hand on her thigh and then uses a 'hand-scooping' wave, which translates as *come here to me*. When she asks me to lie down, she often makes a motion, pushing her right hand from waist high down toward the floor.

When we are playing tug-of-war or fetch with my toys and it's time to stop, she says *all done*, and uses a motion much like a referee uses, sliding her hand across her body, from left to right. I've learned this means *time to go play on your own* . . . so I do.

Until I had all my shots, I wasn't allowed to be among other dogs, so we had teaching-time in the family room every morning. Afterward, I got to go for a ride around the lake in the large basket on the back of her three-wheel bike. The lake's where I learned what ducks, rabbits and other dogs looked like. But no co-mingling yet.

An important pup training tip is to always begin a command with our name: **Romeo**, sit; **Romeo**, wait; **Romeo**, shake hands. Our name gets our attention, and we know the next words are meant specifically for us. Do this *every* time. If there is a lot of conversation going on, we may miss a command. When you use our name first, it's clear that it's our time to listen.

Do you have a lot of endearing extra love names for your dogs? Juliet also calls me "Romes," "Baby Boy," "Pumpkin Pie," and I like hearing those names, but when it comes time for me to obey a command, I am always referred to as "Romeo," and my instructions follow. This little bit of consistency really works.

Spare Us a Scolding

One of the first things I learned was my name. Every time it was spoken, I was encouraged to look up at who was calling me, and run right over to get jolly hugs and pats. This was always such a good feeling and I am so appreciative that I have my own identity.

If we are called over to our master and are scolded or punished when we respond, we will remember that. Those bad memories get in the way of thinking it's a really good thing to come when called, and we pups get confused by this inconsistency.

Separate the issues of punishment from coming when called. When you need to reprimand us, you come to us with our lesson at hand—and do it *immediately*. If too much time passes by between our mistake and the reprimand, we will not understand what is going on.

We naturally want to run to you when you call our name, expecting something very happy and wonderful to happen—always, always. Please make sure that the happy ending always does happen!

Spare Us a Scolding

Our training is much easier and more effective when you take the positive path. Instead of telling us dogs what not to do (which is spending time in the negative), direct us to what you do want us to do. This becomes a natural set-up for praising us.

Instead of saying *no jumping*, say *four on the floor* or *down*. Rather than say *stop it—stop barking at those passing dogs!*, say *heel* and *hush*.

It bears repeating: Please tell us **what to do**, instead of **what NOT to do**.

When I was just nine to ten weeks old at my new home, something happened that gave me the reputation of being highly intuitive and very intelligent (I kind of like being seen this way).

I missed my littermates and mom so much, and I had a lot of separation anxiety when left by myself.

My new master was recovering from a medical situation, and she didn't have the stamina she hoped she would. Raising me, a very active new puppy, was a huge challenge for her at that time, but she was not going to give up.

The breeder had suggested that Juliet get up in the middle of the night to take me outside to potty, as my bladder was so tiny I had to go every few hours. We needed to avoid indoor accidents. For many nights this would interrupt her sleep (which she desperately needed for healing), and when I was taken out, I would not "go."

I barked a lot because I was staying in the master bathroom, and Juliet was in her own bed a few feet away, separated by a baby gate. In my mind, we were way too far away from each other. She was nice and warm, and she would make a good substitute for snuggling between my littermates, my usual way of sleeping until then.

That night, I wore myself out, yipping and barking, hoping against hope that she'd take me into her bed with her.

Juliet was very ill.

She got out of bed at 2 a.m., brought her pillow over to my baby gate, and curled up on the rug, wrapped up in her fuzzy robe.

She said through the bars in the gate, "Romeo, I am really sick and I don't feel good at all. We both need our rest, and you can't bark anymore. I am going to lie down right here beside you, but on my side of the gate. I want you to be a good, quiet boy and go to sleep until morning."

We both put our heads down, and I did not utter a peep for the rest of the night. When we both woke up about 7 a.m., I got the biggest hug you've ever seen.

I slept quietly again the next night, and the next, and every afternoon for our naps, and I never ever barked again during our designated sleeping times. (Yes, she slept in her own bed after that one night.)

All her friends feel I understood something in her voice and delivery that made me want to support her wishes. I did—and I still do. She was now my new world.

Thorns may hurt you, men desert you, sunlight turn to fog; but you're never friendless ever, if you have a dog.

—Douglas Malloch,
American poet (1877-1938)

Just Once

Once I had graduated from my initial puppy training, and had plenty of practice with my obedience lessons, there were new expectations about my behavior.

I loved going to a group training class on the first day, and every week after that. I had never been in an assembly like this before, and oh, boy, I thought it meant play-group time.

Thanks to our terrific trainer, A.J., I soon learned that training class was important business.

As class started, A.J. took my leash from my master's grip because I was being too exuberant. Right then, I saw a twittering bird in a tree, and I didn't hesitate: I barked loudly. Immediately, A.J., slightly tugged at my leash, and in his big masculine voice he boomed, "NO Bark."

I FROZE!

I zipped my mouth shut and did not utter a peep again. My master was amazed; she didn't have that control with me. A.J. explained that her voice was too gentle, so, although it was unnatural for her, she began practicing projecting a more authoritative voice. There's a lot of value in using firmness in your voice when you give commands to us pups.

Two Labradoodle classmates, Presley and Elvis, arrived with their human mom and dad. Presley was six or seven months old, just about my age, and sort of like me—distracted and new to all of this. Even young and distracted, we were good learners because our masters were paying attention. Elvis was older and calmer, knew more about life, and went right along with the program.

This class was a great exercise in socializing. This is where we were taught how to pass by other dogs while we used our good manners. We also had to sit by our masters as they role-played visiting on a street corner. We pups were taught to sit still and patiently while the people chatted. We did not talk to each other or try to play. We got a lot of praise and treats for accomplishing this.

I modestly tell you that I graduated from my class with honors.

Graduation was just the beginning, because I had to continue being a well-behaved dog. Our daily practice continues even years after I graduated. The value of repetition pays off, especially with us dogs. We need ongoing reinforcement and reminding about our manners and commands throughout our lifetime.

Pooches have exceptionally keen hearing, aside from our occasional selective listening. We give our masters respect and show good manners when we respond to their commands the first time. This takes a little extra work.

Canine training emphasizes that commands should

not be repeated: We dogs become confused when a word is repeated, because we're trying to figure out if that is a whole new phrase. It's much more effective to learn to respond the first time we hear our instruction.

Tell us *just once.*

My master gives the command, and then she looks at me and waits until I respond. If I don't act, she silently walks over to me and has me do what I was asked to do—without another word.

For instance, if I was commanded to *sit* (and don't), she lightly taps my hind hip until I do. If I don't *come,* she walks to me, puts her hand in my collar and leads me to the spot where she was standing when she called me over.

I don't like the silent treatment; I would much prefer a reward pat on the head and hearing that familiar, proud tone in her voice, so I really try to act as soon as I hear her speak.

Because she believes in being consistent with the *Just Once!* rule, I know this is how I am expected to respond. Once is enough. This works in my home.

Raise the Praise

We dogs *thrive* on praise, so bring it on in bunches when it's deserved.

Hearing *No!* is not nearly as effective as praise. We think, *What 'no' are you talking about? What are you referring to?*

It's so much better to ignore poor behavior, double up on acknowledging our good actions, and immediately roll out the praises with sincere enthusiasm. (This is a pretty valuable suggestion for two-legged child-rearing as well!)

My new cocker cousin, Ollie, was just rescue-adopted, and his manner-training let him blend right into the family—a real testament to the power of positive reinforcement, even at a later age.

He's a happy camper, who now heels when he's on his walks, always comes when called, and listens well. He learned very quickly because of all the praise and care he received. He's a joyful addition to his family of two cockers, Winston and Penny, and his people-parents.

Raise the Praise

A friend told me a remarkable story about a dog who would never come to his owner when called. When the owner finally hired a trainer to help, the trainer observed the family habits for some time. She noted that the owner was continually reprimanding his dog about a lot of things, using the word 'no' over and over.

The astute trainer asked the owner to call his dog, using the word 'no' as if it were a name. Sure enough, when the owner said "NO, come!" the dog raced right to him.

The poor pooch heard *No!* so often that he thought it was his given name. The owners immediately made some significant, positive changes in their training style. An interesting lesson!

I remember being a young puppy in my new home, and having special lessons in my family room after breakfast every day.

We called it "Home School," and we did it each morning for 10 to 15 minutes. That was just enough time to fit my attention span, and left lots of time to receive tons of praising.

The praise set the stage for my being in a very positive learning environment for evermore. Training has consistently been a fun and happy time, filled with new words, new lessons, and my master being an enthusiastic cheerleader.

Home School is where I learned to shake hands when I heard the command *Romeo, hello!* Now I raise my right paw every time I hear it.

By practicing each morning for a few minutes, within one week I had my handshake down pat. This was pretty much my learning pattern —a week of hearing and being shown a command, a few minutes each day. My jar of training treats got refilled on a very regular basis. Yum!

I say yum, but the truth is, it's not the food that's important; it's the idea and sensation of being rewarded that gets our response. The best treats are tiny for two reasons: We can get lots of them, and we don't have to stop doing what we're doing in order to chew and swallow them.

Four on the Floor

*F*our on the floor! is a nice set of words to define our ideal stature when we greet visitors. This is really a tough one for pooches!

The sound of a doorbell drives most dogs—including me!—into an absolute frenzy. We want to rush to the door and see what's going on. It's not safe, though, for us or whoever is on the other side, and our exuberance needs to be tamed.

Juliet keeps a spare leash at the door. When the doorbell rings, she puts it on me, leads me several feet away from the door, and puts me on a *Romeo, stay!* command. I must sit on that spot, patiently waiting until the visitors come into the house and all the human greetings are done. This is *not* easy!

Humans don't especially like having strange dogs gallop at them and over them, licking, sniffing, and jumping.

From a dog's perspective, it's just our natural instinct to jump up on a human. We are trying to smell the person's breath so we can identify them. It's the same reason we sniff crotches; everything is in the scent for us, and it tells us who you are and if we've met before.

I know it's considered obnoxious by humans, and a real turn-off, but please be patient with us, because we can be taught the good manners of not doing this type of profiling.

I naturally want to show an enthusiastic *Hello!* to people entering my home, but I have learned to keep all four feet on the ground. If I don't, I won't get greeted and petted by them. I really do want to be courteous.

It takes time to learn this command. If I jump up when people arrive, they are coached to turn their back on me and ignore me until I settle down and get all four paws back on the floor.

Some dogs are the quiet-silent type and may not bark at the sound of a ding-dong. Instead, they're focused on the idea of protecting the house, and they'll approach the door with the idea that there's an intruder trying to come in.

You can teach a dog to bark on command, especially if you want the person on the outside of the door to know you have a "fierce" guard dog with you on the inside.

Four on the floor works for more than just greeting visitors. When I roam around the food-prep section of the kitchen, I am always reminded where my four paws belong.

If I put my front paws up on sofas and chairs, *four on the floor* reminds me I need to back off.

I have a human godmommie, Nancy, and every time we are together it's a royal love-fest. I love her so much! She is very fit and practices Pilates in her living room. In one of her routines, she lies flat on the floor and as she slowly begins to sit up, she raises her arms over her head. When I visit her, I like to lie down beside her during this workout.

As I watch this exercise, I reach up with my front paw and place it on her forearm, forcing her arm back down to the floor. I did this so often, that she decided to wait to exercise until I took my nap. I was just trying to teach her the important manner of paws on the floor.

I think I am catching on to this paw rule, and here is one clue: Without being prompted, I have become the morning wake-up call to my master. I seem to have my own inner-clock. There are theories about dogs being time keepers, but no one is quite sure why or how we can do this yet.

I don't know either, but I've been told that more research is being done. Here is what I have fun doing, while being a good boy because I do it with no reminder of where my four paws should be placed.

If Juliet is not up by 6:30 a.m., I walk over to her bedside at 6:31 each morning, and keep all four paws on the floor. I'd like to put my two front paws up on her bed, but I don't. I want to start the day off right.

I place my long nose on her bed by her pillow and look right into her face. Juliet always gives me a big hello smile, a pat on my fluffy head, and says "*Bon jour, Romeo. Merci!*" That's all the French I know so far.

Fashionable, Functional Neckwear

Going outside into the fresh air is the best activity ever. Because many of us are town dogs, we can't romp through our communities leashless. A collar and a leash are essential accessories for us.

Our masters spend a bit of time selecting certain sporty colors and styles for these items. They seem to care about that much more than we do.

My Orange County retriever pal, Dallas, has a full selection of scarves he wears in addition to his collar. His master is a fashionista, so it's not surprising that his neckwear collection is extensive—prints and patterns for every holiday, season, and fun occasion. I only have scarves for the Fourth of July, St. Patrick's Day, and a 5K that I walked one time.

For us, getting used to having something around our neck is one more lesson we need to abide by. We need to wear our I.D. tags and license whenever we're in public. Being identifiable is a good enough reason to wear our neckbands.

When it's time to take a walk, it is helpful if we cooperate by sitting still while our collar and leash are put on. Putting us on a *sit-stay* command is usually the simplest way.

When I don't co-operate, my master stops trying, puts my leash down, and waits for me to settle down. She's aware of just how much I enjoy our walks, and she knows I'll agree to her command soon. She holds firm. Eventually, I get the idea and allow her to put the gear on. This is a message I get from her all the time, so I've learned to just do what she asks. The payoff is always good!

Check with your trainer or pet shops to see what type of collar is best for your dog. The traditional nylon or leather will work for many canines. You'll know you have the right size when you can just slip two fingers between your dog's neck and the collar.

You may want more than one style.

Harnesses are especially helpful if your dog has any trachea issues or sensitive neck problems. Harnesses are also helpful if you'd like your dog to pull you while you're on your bike or skateboard (careful—that can be dangerous).

The Gentle Leader collar gives the master great control, and as the name suggests, gently. A part of this collar loops over the dog's nose and connects directly to the leash, and there's a lot less pulling.

A slip collar is good for dogs that are easily distracted, because it can be used for quick corrections.

I have a couple of buddies who are pretty strong (and strong-willed), and they wear chain slip collars or chain prong collars. These models are often used during training to tell a dog it's time to pay serious attention.

The collars aren't harmful; they are constant reminders to listen to your commands. You'll often see them on large or muscular dogs who can pull a lot of weight.

If you do a lot of walking in the dark, think about collars and leashes that are reflectorized; that can be a great safety measure.

If money is no object, there are some new collars with built-in GPS and training tones that work with the master's smartphone.

While your leash choice is mostly based on style and budget, it's necessary to consider the size and personality of your dog, too. Smaller dogs don't need a thick, heavy leash, but larger dogs prone to pulling might require a stronger leash for better control. If you have any doubts, ask a pet professional for advice.

Straight, or standard, leashes are available in a variety of widths, lengths, and colors, and most feature a loop at the end for easy gripping. They're made of nylon, leather, and even reflective fabric for night safety.

Retractable leashes usually feature a thick plastic grip, with a thin nylon cord that comes out when pulled and retracts when the pressure is released, like a measuring tape. Most include an override button that can lock the release mechanism. These leashes can work against you when teaching loose-leash walking and are not permitted during Canine Good Citizen tests.

Whichever style of collar and leash you select, your most effective tool is the body language that you, as our master, use when you walk us. We feel your authority when you stand very tall, keep your head up, shoulders back, and speak like an alpha dog. We'll follow you anywhere!

Wait at the Gate and Door

We furry creatures are grateful that our owners want to keep us safe. It's important to teach us to *Wait!* on command at an open doorway to the outside, and at gates that lead out to a busy street. This also protects passers-by from being lunged at because we're anxious to play.

I learned the *wait* command easily, as my master consistently said *Romeo, wait!* while I was on my leash inside our door. When she says, *Romeo, okay!*, then I walk out the door or through the gate.

When I come to a curb, she says, *Romeo, wait!* As soon as the way is clear of cars, pedestrians, and bikes, she says *Romeo, cross!* Off we prance.

I am also expected to sit and wait when we go to our mailbox. It's sometimes a challenge, because lizards, other pets, and kids on skate boards are passing by, and I want to join them. Often, I am given a small cookie treat to thank me for sitting still while Juliet unlocks our mail box and collects the envelopes.

Wait at the Gate and Door

As eager as I am to get out of the car when we arrive at our destination, I've been taught to *Wait!* there too. I always sit in the back seat. I'm told that is the safest place in an automobile for most dogs to be. Small dogs should ride in a crate in the back seat; they can be crushed by the air bags if there's an accident when they're in the front seat. If the ride is longer than a few minutes, it's a good idea to have some water and a bowl handy.

My best poodle buddy and mentor is Cooper; his coat has turned charcoal grey now that he is nine. I try to copy everything he does. He is a marathon walker and still has a huge amount of pep in his step. He taught me how to sit right by the doggy-treat cupboard door and be persistent. When we ride to the dog park in the same car, we sit in the back seat together. We look like two dudes sitting tall, side by side, just ready to go out and romp. When we arrive at our destination and the car door is opened, we wait for our *Okay!* command before we leap out.

It's risky to let a dog ride with its head out of an open window. Besides the possibility of foreign objects damaging our eyes and ears, our urge to leap out when spotting a cat or something wonderful to chase is a dangerous possibility. In some states, it's illegal for a dog to ride with its head out of a window.

You may shop for the many types of dog restraints available, from harnesses, to safe leashes, booster seats, vests, and belts. You wouldn't have a child in the car without protection; please don't let your furry child be unsecured. Not only might we turn into a projectile in an accident (often going through the windshield), we will be panicked and are likely to run out into traffic if an EMT or police officer opens the door after a crash.

Wait at the Gate and Door

We all should know the hazards of leaving us in the car unattended. Within ten minutes, the temperature in a car can reach a lethal level, either too hot or too freezing—even if the outside temp seems comfortable to you humans. Dogs have a very different and more vulnerable body temperature control than humans. We can suffer from shock, heatstroke, or hypothermia very easily.

Please *never* leave us alone in your car. This is a really good reason to train us to be well mannered, so that we can join you outside the car and be welcome most places you go.

A Message of Friendly

Yippee! I see more playmates coming toward me. I think everyone will like me and be my friend—but that is not always the case.

Because I'm a big dog and stand tall, I learned that if I sit very still on the sidewalk with a smile on my face, then I send out a message to oncoming dogs and people that I am NO THREAT. It works *almost* every time.

If very small dogs are headed my way, I like to lie down, and they seem very comfortable with that posture. My little Cavalier King Charles girlfriend Ruby just rolls over next to me when I do this, and she caresses me.

Our masters have a big part in our socialization. If they are afraid or nervous of other dogs—guess what?—we absorb their emotion.

If they are confident and encourage our social encounters, we have a better experience and more trust when we meet new fur-pals.

I've heard that some dogs are size-blind, and without thinking about another dog's enormity or puniness,

A Message of Friendly

they begin a relationship on the spot. I think we know how to look for inner beauty.

Almost every morning, I walk by our two neighborhood beagle boys, Elwood the introvert, who glances quickly and continues with sniff-patrol, and Dodger the extrovert, who likes more interaction and wags his tail as he enjoys my master's pat on his head. These beagles qualify for our Good Manners team with their kind, relaxed greetings.

There are a few really super people who walk the same paths we do, and they know how to make us grin. They carry dog treats in their pockets all the time. These gems of humanity are very considerate and cautious; they always ask our masters if we're allowed to have a cookie before they treat us. We *never* turn them down.

I totally agree with the saying I heard once, "If you think

dogs can't count, put three biscuits in your pocket and then give them only two."

Unfortunately, sometimes we'll be enjoying a happy walk and lots of cheery greetings, then, darn it, a dog will pass me on the pathway with the meanest growl, a lunge, and a vicious look. There is no excuse for this behavior; it's plain rude. They should report for training duty.

I won't respond to a mean dog's unfriendly behavior, because Juliet has observed the situation ahead of time. She's already said, in her assured tone, *Romeo, no visit!*, and she keeps us walking as we just ignore that anti-social dog. After we pass, she praises me for being such a gentleman.

Dogs can be taught to behave in a civilized, friendly way, and it makes life more relaxed and pleasant for all of us—dogs *and* humans.

Sidewalk Garden-Pardons

I'm clueless about the rules regarding where I should and shouldn't lift my leg when we're on our walks. That's why it's good that we have considerate and aware humans on the other end of our leashes at all times.

While we walk through neighborhoods with pretty gardens, we are not supposed to tromp through the flowerbeds and ruin beautifully planted yards. Usually there is a plain grassy strip on the street side of the sidewalk, and that's the mannerly place for us to do our business. Our pee is lethal to green lawns. Girl dogs, especially, can make a big brown dead spot with one pee.

We learn a good habit if our masters gently guide our leashes to that plain grassy strip and regularly encourage us to potty there. I even get praised for pottying (outside!), so, you see, there are no boundaries how we can earn congratulations.

Please pardon us if nature calls and we make a mistake—we usually try our best to use unlandscaped places.

Most all masters do a good job of picking up after us. That's what all those puffy plastic bags you see tied around our leashes are for!

While we walk, we often try to help clean up your environs by thoughtfully picking up dirty Kleenex, food wrappers, dead birds, and other messes. I hear my master say something like *oh, yuk,* and then she gives me the command *Romeo, leave it!* That means I am supposed to ignore that delectable item I was sniffing, and keep on walking.

If she doesn't catch me before I snatch it up and it's already between my teeth, I'm supposed to drop it immediately. At first, she had to pull it from my mouth (that's why she carries a small bottle of antibacterial disinfectant—for *her* hands), but now I get it, and I am praised for being a good listener and not picking up those delectables.

Juliet and I never leave the house for a walk without looking like two scouts headed out on a cross-country hike. She wears a hat for sun protection, and she always has her walking purse with a cross-shoulder strap, which holds all our essentials. It makes garden touring easier to have everything we need at our finger and paw tips.

In addition to the hand disinfectant, she carries essential items: our identification papers, a little bit of money, our house key, cell phone for emergencies, pepper spray (more about that later), and a couple of treats for me. Of course, we never go anywhere without several plastic potty bags. Did you know some are scented? (They're really nice.) If it's warm or we're going on a long walk, we carry a water bottle. Being scout-prepared has its benefits.

I mentioned the pepper spray; we carry it to protect us from coyotes and any other dangers that approach us. The containers come in various sizes and they spray different distances. Pepper gel is a good choice, because it reaches out 30 feet and won't blow back on you on a windy day. Testimonials from fellow dog owners tell us that this is a reliable deterrent to problem situations.

Our travel bag helps us safely go anywhere we want to walk—along our neighborhood sidewalks and gardens, paseos and trails, and beyond.

Polite Compromises

There are a few points of view on whether dog walking should be all walking and no sniffing, or unlimited sniffing, or a little of each. That's for each family to decide on their own.

Because I don't have a yard and spend most of my outdoor time on the end of the leash, my master and I have compromised and I get both. I would say I probably do 49% walking and 51% sniffing.

For us canines, sniffing is second only to oxygen. We can't breathe without it.

When we start our walks, I am given the whole long leash to use and the command, *Go sniff!* Now I can whirl and twirl until I find my perfect spot to do my potty business, and I fully enjoy the freedom of being outside. This is lizard-alert time, sniffing out squirrels in the trees, exploring nature at its best.

The second half of the walk is on a *Heel!* command, and I am very cooperative since I've gotten the rush of curious-exploring out of my system. I'm a little calmer and can stay more focused.

Polite Compromises

I hear people say that for us dogs, sniffing is like reading the morning paper; we get all the local news that way. We know who has been where before us, how tall or short they were, if they were big or little critters, their state of health, and pretty much all we need to know.

Here's an insightful tale for you: Several doggy cousins of mine, Barney, Gracie, Talulah, Denali, and Olive, were sitting around a fire hydrant chatting. Barney told the others, "Rover down the street has moved away, and Rosie next door just had a new litter of pups." All these dogs wanted to know how he knew this. Barney answered with a shrug, "I read my pee-mail this morning." This is a true story—probably.

While I was a young pup in my first training class, we were taught the command *Heel!* I don't know what got into me, but when we practiced that command on real walks, I sat down on the sidewalk and would not budge. (Maybe I thought when my master said "heel," she was calling me a scoundrel.) I did it so often, Juliet became concerned and called the veterinarian, wondering if I could be in pain. The truth was just that I can be stubborn, and just do not like being bossed sometimes.

She let it go for a while, and did not press it.

Then one day she used a different word along with a treat. Juliet said, *Romeo, WALKING!* while holding my leash close by her side. She also had a very alpha-tone to her voice. I happily followed her that day, and she awarded me a pat on the head and a treat, and then another, and another. I liked this, and now I am heeling like a champ, but with our agreed-upon new word—just a simple *walking!*

Polite compromises work out very well most of the time.

Hark the Bark

Our barks are worth a lot, and this we know. Humans know the value of a barking dog to deter crimes and generally alert them. But like humans who like to hear themselves talk, sometimes we get noisy just for fun.

Listen carefully to the sound and tone of our barks. The lighter and higher the pitch, the more playful and conversational our bark is. The deeper and louder it is, the more of a safety warning it is. This goes for growls too. We must not be discouraged from being good guard dogs, but we can also learn when *not* to bark—on command.

When we are on walks and pass other dogs on the sidewalk, we can be taught a polite *No bark!* A quick tug at the leash at the same time and then praise will eventually show results. A reward treat really helps us learn better and faster, too.

If the master is calm and assured while passing other dogs on the path, we will follow suit. This is one of the best signs of canine etiquette. Give us lots of praise when we have successfully passed another dog on the path—quietly.

It's also good manners to not scare the ducks and geese along our path. My master uses the command *No visit!,* and that means that I am supposed to walk straight, calmly, right beside her, and with no change in my pace as I pass other animals, dogs, and some people. This makes for very amicable relationships in the neighborhood.

When we are trying to warn our masters with a bark, another phrase they can say back to us is *Good alert!* (pause about 3 seconds), then say *Release!* This tells us that we have done something very important as a watch dog, and now we do not need to continue barking. Our warning has been duly noted.

Good alert . . . release! supports and encourages our natural instinct of wanting to protect.

Lucy, my adorable havanese friend, is trying so hard to learn this phrase. Her master says that Lucy thinks she is being told *good alert . . . repeat!* She'll get it when she is ready.

Cheers for Ears

Speaking of ears, using ours is part of our everyday job. Dogs' ears are so acutely sensitive that we can hear human heartbeats, and we count them! Yes, we are counting your heartbeats . . . who knew!

When your heartbeat accelerates, diminishes, or changes, that alerts us. Pretty awesome, isn't it! This is one way we detect fear or anxiety in you, can tell when you're joyful, and also know when you become ill.

It goes without saying that we dogs try to ward off danger when we hear something wrong. Recently, Juliet and I had an intruder at our front gate, which we keep locked at night.

At the pitch-dark time just before dawn, I smelled and heard someone out front. I left my bed and trotted over to my master with the strangest growl/bark she had ever heard come out of my mouth. It awakened her, but drowsily she fell back asleep.

A couple hours later when we went out for our daily morning walk, she could not unlock our front gate—the lock had been jimmied and jammed with something like a screw driver. She realized that I had caught the scent and sound of an intruder just two hours before, and my bark had scared him away. She vowed to me that she would forever pay very close attention to the signals I give her.

Everything we canines do has meaning. It's a learning curve for both us and our masters to understand the communications we exchange. The attitude of gratitude that our humans have for us and our alertness is indeed part of sensitive civility. No matter what our lineage, we dogs want to repay the love we receive from you, many times over. Yes, we've got the beat!

If we are making too much noise, and you yell back at us with a very loud voice, we think you're setting an example, and you're encouraging us to talk even louder. We assume you're barking back at us. How cool! We're natural mimics, so what we hear is what we do: bark back even louder than before.

So, if you want us to be quiet, tell us in a very soft tone. You can even use the command *Hush!* and hold your index finger across your mouth when it's time for us to be considerately quiet. We like hand signals, too, and that is another way to direct us at certain times.

My Yorkipoo pal, Dudley, has very big ears for such a small dog. Every day at specific times, he waits and listens by the living room window, knowing the neighboring kids will be walking by to or from school. His inner clock knows just when to expect that activity.

When it's close to that time, he goes to his master and gives a special look, which is his signal asking to please be taken out on his leash to the front yard to socialize with these jolly little humans. He is referred to as "The Mayor" by all his neighborly friends. Dudley is a pro at well-mannered greetings.

When it comes to our ability to listen to you, much of our attitude and response has to do with the tone and inflection in your voice.

My ears are very tuned in to my master's tone of voice. If she uses her stern voice peppered with a bit of impatience, it turns me off and I don't mind her.

When she uses her soft, happy melodic voice, she has me in the palm of her hand; I'll do anything for her. She says I've taught her a thing or two about life.

Doggy Dining Etiquette

The best possible way to figure out a good dining schedule is for a dog and master to work it out together. One style doesn't fit every dog. A common method is to feed at very specific times, and pick up any uneaten food after a certain period of time.

That doesn't work for me. *I* am a grazer, and since it was apparent from the beginning that I was not a chow-hound, we settled on an open-grazing pattern.

I like to eat later in the day. During the daytime, if my master goes out alone on errands and social appointments, she gives me a treat—a healthy nutritious chew-bone. First, I must earn that food with a 'sit'. Then she thanks me for guarding the house while she is gone, and we are good to go.

Being asked to sit before we get our food is a reinforcing habit. It helps us appreciate and respect our home life, value the nourishment we receive, and it's an extra bonding moment between dog and master.

Jazz, one of my first lakeside buddies, is a most

handsome silver-beige Standard Poodle. We give each other the *'I want to play'* bow when we pass by on our walks.

In his puppy era, he was taught to sit before his parents put food in his bowl. Now he sits without being asked. He also sits to tell them when he is hungry before mealtime, or to suggest he'd like another helping. This is a family of true communicators.

If you folks want a calm mealtime yourself, without us begging at your chair, *never, ever* start giving us tidbits from your table. Once you start, our memory won't let us or you forget that heavenly happening.

We are very healthy on a pure dog food diet, and we don't need your people food. In fact, people food can be harmful to our digestive tracts, and at times even fatal. There are online lists you can reference for dog-dangerous foods.

That said, there are some foods that you eat that we can enjoy and thrive on as well, and you can also find those listed online. We are told that certain raw vegetables are good for us, as well salmon, pumpkin, sweet potatoes, eggs, unsweetened yogurt and more. It's still to your advantage that all the human foods be placed in our food bowl, not given to us from your plate.

If you see that your pet has a tendency or a beginning habit to beg at your lap, put him in a lay down command, off to the side, during your mealtime.

Leaving food on counters is not fair to your four-legged friends. Some temptations are greater than any good canine citizen can bear. Please help us be good dogs by not putting alluring food within our reach. Sometimes we have self-restraint, but often it's beyond our control to ignore the impulse to wolf down a hearty morsel of your tempting food.

We can be pretty creative when it comes to getting to that food. My out-of-state friend Beauregard, a sweet, innocent-looking bichon frisé, used bar stools to climb onto the kitchen counter and steal an entire rotisserie chicken, still in its plastic clamshell case. He hauled it the length of the house onto his masters' bed, where he opened the container and ate the hot chicken, bones and all. Fortunately, nothing suffered but the bedspread.

Nibbling on random and unmeasured human food can also lead to our becoming fat. Extra fat on dogs shortens our lifespan and causes all kinds of pain and disease, from hip disease to cancer.

Going out to a restaurant for dinner is almost as special for us as it is for you humans. Even though we don't order, this is when our dining etiquette must be at its best.

I like places where the wait staff welcomes us with big smiles and a sense of friendliness and brings us a water dish. Even though I don't share the food, I do enjoy all the gourmet smells and the different under-the-table sights. I can always count on being given a doggy treat while my master is eating her meal.

My master reminds me of her expectations as soon as we sit down: I am to sit or lie down quietly, and not wander or wrap my leash around her chair.

Another good friend named Beau is one of my frequent restaurant companions. He is also a poodle, but in a miniature size, and he is a great example. He does not bark one peep when out in a public eating establishment. He is a star when it comes to knowing all about being mannerly savvy—and this is one reason he is also invited to go to movies. He's quite debonair.

Apartment Pooches

Charlie, my Labradoodle buddy, invites me to his home and backyard for playdates. It's a real treat to roam free in a safe, fenced grassy area.

There's also a pool out there, but since Charlie never shows interest in jumping in, I just figured I'd follow his lead and consider that off limits.

He taught me to go in and out of a doggy door. I had no idea what that was until I watched him push through it, and it quickly became a cool activity.

This kind of play is such a happy good time for an "apartment pooch," a term I use to include all pets who live in townhomes, condos, and any places that do not have fenced, safe outdoor yard space where we can run around without a leash.

If we pay attention to our visiting manners, we will probably get invited more often for the type of social outings that I enjoy with Charlie.

A dog park becomes the standby recreation place for many apartment pooches. I know some masters aren't comfortable taking their dogs there, as they are skeptical of various dog behaviors, disease, and other issues. That is understandable, yet there are many benefits, if you're careful.

We poodles are athletes with extremely long legs, and we thrive on running around like racehorses and playing and wrestling with other dogs. We also like the mental stimulation of agility courses. For this reason, Juliet and I try to make dog parks work for us.

Both my master and I work together to assess if a dog park is a safe place each time we visit. We *wait, watch* and *assess* before entering, and we always bring my own water bottle. Usually I meet and greet very playful, friendly dogs, and we rumble and tumble all over the pen.

My master never takes her eyes off me and what I am doing the whole time we are there. She assesses the other dogs, too. That is what all dog owners are expected to do when visiting these places.

One day I did not feel like engaging with the other two dogs who were in a dog park. They were a little too aggressive, and their play did not seem friendly. After I trotted around the grounds on my own for a while, digging and doing some exploring, I needed to decide if I wanted to join the other dogs. I thought about it, and it still didn't feel right, so I walked over to Juliet and just stood quietly by her side.

She could not believe what she was seeing; it'd never happened before. In fact, most days she could barely rein me in when it was time to leave. I stood still, and positioned my body facing the exit, my head focused on the gate. She read my body language, quickly clipped on my leash, and off we went. We were a good team that day. Paying attention is critical.

When you play games with us and entertain us with our toys, that is another activity that we apartment pooches look forward to. Even if it's only five minutes a day, we feel *great* about our interaction. It's a special connecting time.

With neighboring walls very close by, we can show good manners and consideration by keeping our mindless barking to a minimum. If our master's voice telling us to be quiet is louder than our barks, that's double trouble. Both of us have to be aware and cooperate.

Going to malls is another great outing, and it's especially helpful on rainy days or scorching hot afternoons. This is an excellent way to get our exercise with the bonus of recording new indoor scents and seeing so many intriguing sights.

Everybody wants to pet me while I am mall-strolling.

Many people don't realize they should always ask our masters first—they should get permission to pet us. This gives everyone involved time to adjust, so no one (pooch *or* person) is taken off guard, or surprised, or stressed. Some dogs should never be petted: service dogs, police dogs and other working dogs.

Brainy Games

When we offer you one of our toys, we are saying *I love you!* Since our playthings are important to us, sharing them with you is a sincere message of bonding.

My master is teaching me the names of my various toys. You should see the smile on her face when she asks me to fetch one of them by name, and I dig in my toy box and bring out the one she has named. Juliet's so impressed and excited that she acts like a zany cheerleader. I like that, so I keep playing along with her.

We pups *love* to be mentally stimulated and challenged. It will keep us out of mischief, since if we are bored, we may feel the need to rip the sofa, chew on the leg of a chair, or get into trouble. A bored dog is a destructive dog. Keeping us challenged with brainy games is so much better for us and for your furniture and shoes.

Another stimulating mental and physical exercise for dogs is taking them to agility classes and agility courses. All levels of skill are welcome, and venues range from private farms to your local park and recreation department. As a bonus, we get socializing time with other dogs at these events, meeting and sniffing before and after class, and at the end of a routine.

Being a community volunteer is another positive way to support mental and social stimulation for us dogs. Applying for a certificate to become a registered Therapy Dog, which is what I am, has such terrific benefits. A simplified definition of a Therapy Dog is a 'visiting dog.' We are different from Service Dogs, who assist people with disabilities.

R.E.A.D. stands for "Reading Education Assistance Dogs"—that's me, too! When I'm dressed up with my designated red collar, red woven leash, and red scarf with the R.E.A.D. logo on it, I know I'm about to visit one of the local libraries in the community where I live. It's time for me to go to work.

When we're working at the library, we are loved by

all the people we meet: the young student readers, their parents, and the library staff. The school district appreciates us too; this is a helpful, well-received national program that improves children's love for books. Teachers report that reading scores are going up, thanks in part to this program.

My master puts my blanket down in the designated reading area, and she and I sit on it. It's red and black with dog paw prints, naturally!

The children select the books they want to read out loud (I laugh, because usually they choose books about dogs), then a child joins me on the blanket, sits, and reads to me. I'm the listener—that's my job. While the children read, they often hold my paw, or pet my fur.

This is when I must be very mannerly and respectful. I pay attention and listen quietly to the children, even though I have a *huge* urge to play with them. These smiling kids relax, do not feel inhibited about reading, and they never feel judged, because they see in our eyes how much we like being with them.

Before my readers leave, I give them each a bookmark with my picture on it, and invite them to come back soon. They love this very simple little gift—and I love them.

Another favorite job is visiting the Memory Care Center, which is part of a new assisted living community in town. Several other of my therapy dog buddies will be there, too, and we rotate around the large social room and take turns visiting with the residents. As they talk to us and pet us, we watch their eyes light up and their smiles widen from ear to ear.

We are trained to stay very calm in this room, and we are not allowed to interact with the other dogs. We are there to work! We rest our noses in the residents' laps and sometimes right in their hands, and we get the best pettings ever. I just rest my head carefully and listen as my master has sweet conversations with the ladies and gentlemen who live there.

Out into the Big World

The huge benefit of being socialized and having good manners is being able to accompany our masters into the big world. It's a tremendous pleasure for both us dogs and our humans, and we don't take it for granted. It's hard work getting there.

I was exposed to many experiences, took training classes, and did my daily home schooling. When I was trusted to obey commands and respond safely, I earned the privilege of going out into the community on an almost-daily basis.

It feels like a graduation when all our learning pays off—and off we trot to lots of big-world places.

As a well-mannered dog, I accompany Juliet to the post office, the bank, to retail stores, to restaurants that are pet-friendly, to malls, to medical centers, libraries, beaches, overnights to friends' homes, business offices, and anywhere that's fun and appropriate.

When visiting buildings where elevators are needed, dog elevator etiquette is important to know. We always stand back, away from the door, and give the people coming off the elevators plenty of room to exit before we enter calmly.

As we walk into the elevator, we move to the back and I sit immediately. Just because I like everyone, it doesn't mean that everyone likes or trusts me and other dogs. We must all be aware of people's concerns, and stay very close to our master's side while we're using these large steel "moving boxes."

Melek is my worldly pup-pal who has traveled greater distances than a lot of people I know. She's an Anatolian mixed shepherd, and she was born in Istanbul, Turkey. When Melek was three months old, she was rescued by a flight attendant and flown to the United States to be adopted. She's a good one to pass on a few travel tips.

She knows that travel etiquette is really important, as

it keeps a trip running smoothly. No matter where we roam, whether it's near home or somewhere else in the world, everyone appreciates good traveling behavior by pets and their owners.

Melek makes sure her ID tags are always on, and she packs documents showing that all her shots are up to date.

The same common-sense advice applies for airplane flights: Have all required documents handy, check pet policies with the airlines, make the carrier crate as cozy and familiar as possible, and get some exercise ahead of time.

There's always a crate in her car or recreational vehicle, just in case certain conditions warrant it. Her family checks ahead of time to be sure the places they are staying welcome pets and notes details of the pet policies. Last-minute surprises are no fun.

Melek is such a girly-girl, she packs all her favorites: towels that smell like home, her decorative doggie bowls, her best blanket, toys she likes, some treats and chew toys, water bottles, even flea and tick meds. She likes to bathe at home, so she always does that just before departing; she never uses the hotel tub (not a good idea).

Melek almost never makes a mess, and if she does, her family cleans everything up right away. She does not bark much, and tries to be as quiet as possible because of nearby strangers. She does not damage her hotel room rug or furniture because she is rarely left unattended.

To avoid any accidents when we're in buildings, please always potty us first before we go inside. Just to be safe, tuck a piece of paper towel and a plastic potty bag into your pocket.

The English translation of her Turkish name is *Angel*—

that sure fits! It's important to Melek to set a good example out there for us while she is vacationing. She has paved the way for us, showing how easy it is to bring pets along on trips, and making it fun and comfortable for everyone involved.

Even humans say that no matter how exciting it is to get away, it's always divine to come home to the comforts of their own houses.

I agree! My toy box, my crate, my sofa, my sunny front porch, my pals, and all my familiar scents—they miss me, too.

So, here's to the joys of how we live, both out in the big world and in our own personal world, with the people we love. Did you know that a dog wags its tail with its heart?

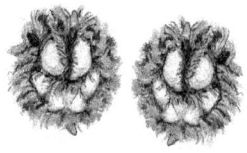

Manners! Shmanners! So, what's the big deal?

My senses tell me that if we pay attention to our neck of the woods and act with civility, our own little world is the best place of all to kick-start a happy, romping, sniffing good life.

Using good manners all the time may keep our world, which begins with our own front yards, from having tussles, perhaps even big conflicts or wars.

Are you in? Let's do it! Woofs, cheers, and paws-up to using as many good manners as we and our partners—furry and otherwise—can handle.

> **On the day God created dogs,**
> **He sat down and smiled.**

About the Coauthors

Juliet, as she's nicknamed by her friends, is also known as Louise Elerding, author of an award-winning series of books for children, *You've Got Manners!* The books include etiquette tips for human readers from three to ninety-three on table manners, social pointers, and how to be more tactful in life.

Juliet/Louise agreed to be Romeo's writing hands for this book, as his paws have trouble using a keyboard.

Romeo is her proud canine partner, and together they have accomplished his certification as a registered Therapy Dog. His volunteer work includes visiting patients at the Oakmont Memory Care Center in Valencia, and participating in the R.E.A.D. program at the libraries in Santa Clarita Valley.

Romeo and Juliet/Louise live happily in Valencia, California, knowing that their meeting was no accident. They enjoy watching the growing awareness and enthusiasm in both canines and people who support and join the Polite Team of the Canine World.

Other books written by Louise Elerding:
Gold Recipient of MOM'S CHOICE AWARDS:
Illustrated Series:
You've Got Manners!
A series of books for kids of any age:

Tactful Tips from A to Z for Kids of All Ages

Table Tips from A to Z for Kids of All Ages

Party Pointers from A to Z for Kids of All Ages

Ya Tienes Buenos Modales

Pass the Manner, Please (card game)

To order the *You've Got Manners* titles or additional copies of this book, visit Amazon.com. For autographed copies of any of these titles, contact **MannersA2Z@aol.com**

www.ingramcontent.com/pod-product-compliance
Lightning Source LLC
Chambersburg PA
CBHW070647050426
42451CB00008B/306